Janet — I hope you will enjoy
this book and find it as comforting as I did
and I know how much you enjoy the sea
and the beach too!

Love,
Mary Ellen

Love is measured not in moments of time...
but in timeless moments.

— Robert W. Lawrence

Acknowledgments

To my sister, Bobbie Hamblet Wilkinson, and my mother, Mae Hamblet,
who have always encouraged me to keep building my sandcastles.

To my family and friends, who have taught me there is no limit to the
human spirit and to what faith can see us through.

To Chip MacGregor, Alive Communications, and Harvest House Publishers,
for your constant support and encouragement.

To the Lord, who continues to shower me with blessings
and with messages from His beautiful shore.

Dedication

In loving memory of my beloved father, Newt Hamblet, and to my beautiful mother, Mae Hamblet,
who have been a lifelong source of inspiration to me and who taught me, by example, how to
create precious "sandcastle moments," no matter what obstacles might appear.

To my dear husband, Steve, who is a wonderful sandcastle builder...thank you for teaching me how to
soar in the midst of adversity...for being an inspiration to me every day and the maker of all my dreams.

To Kristin, Todd, Kevin, and Amanda Adams...who continually bless me
and make my heart smile. I am honored to be your mom.

To Bobbie and Tom Wilkinson, Janice, Kenny and Shirley Hamblet, Doreen Croson,
Sue Breen, and Shelley Little...thank you for the richness you all bring to my life.

To my aunt, Judy Hamblet, whose love, support, and passion for living inspire me daily.

To Paula Correia, Riley Cunningham, Ray LaRocque, Pam Mikulis, and Rich Nobile...
your courage, spirit, and ability to live each day to the fullest continue to make
a beautiful difference in my life.

To Nancy and Rick Booms, Ellen and Bill Goodchild, Margaret and Patrick Nassaney, and Sally
White...thank you for showing me how to go on again...how to believe again...
how to build sandcastles again.

To all of our brave men and women who protect and serve our country and our world every
day so that we may be free to create "sandcastle moments." God bless you all.

My Beautiful Sandcastle Moments

Carol Hamblet Adams

Paintings by

Gay T. Boassy

HARVEST HOUSE PUBLISHERS

EUGENE, OREGON

My Beautiful Sandcastle Moments

Text copyright © 2004 by Carol Hamblet Adams
Published by Harvest House Publishers
Eugene, Oregon 97402
www.harvesthousepublishers.com

Library of Congress Cataloging-in-Publication Data
Adams, Carol Hamblet, 1943-
My beautiful sandcastle moments / Carol Hamblet Adams ; paintings by Gay Talbott Boassy.
   p. cm.
ISBN 0-7369-1189-8 (alk. paper)
1. Consolation. I. Title.
BV4905.3.A333 2003
242—dc22

2003015525

Published in association with the literary agency of Alive Communications, Inc., 7680 Goddard Street, Suite 200,
Colorado Springs, CO 80920.

Carol Hamblet Adams is a writer and motivational speaker who has had a lifelong love of the ocean. She lives in
Southeastern Massachusetts and on Cape Cod. Carol gives keynote addresses, seminars, and retreats, and she can
be reached at P.O. Box 1388, Attleboro Falls, MA 02763-0388 or at carol@carolhambletadams.com.

All works of art reproduced in the book are copyrighted by Gay Talbott Boassy and may not be reproduced without the artist's permission. For more information regarding art featured in this book, please contact: Gay Talbott
Boassy, 474 Comanche Trail, Lawrenceville, GA 30044, (770) 979-8281.

Design and production by Koechel Peterson & Associates, Inc., Minneapolis, Minnesota.

Printed in China.

04 05 06 07 08 09 10 11 12 13 / IM / 10 9 8 7 6 5 4 3 2 1

Preface

In 1982, when my husband, Steve, was diagnosed with multiple sclerosis, so many valuable lessons came to me from the Lord. At the beach that summer, I watched Steve go to the shore and build beautiful sandcastles all day long. I couldn't believe he was carefree enough to do this when so many heavy burdens were weighing our hearts down. The last thing I wanted to do was build a sandcastle that would only be taken away by the tide. I was much too busy worrying about tomorrow to enjoy the beauty of today.

But Steve continued to build his sandcastles…not worrying about the changing tides of his life. He continued to build his dreams…to claim hope and joy.

Many years have passed since that day on the beach. Steve continues to build sandcastles…and I have learned one of my life's most important lessons. When we have an opportunity to create a very special memory…to share time with a loved one…to cherish the miracle of "now"…to build a dream…even if it is only for a brief moment, we need to take that chance and truly appreciate it. For we don't know when the tide will come and wash that opportunity…that dream…that person…away.

It is my prayer that *My Beautiful Sandcastle Moments* will help you to stop each day—no matter what is going on in your life—and appreciate the joy and the precious beauty of "now"… if only for a moment.

Beside restful waters He leads me; He refreshes my soul.

Psalm 23:2

The rush of a summer breeze rustles the crisp
white bedroom curtains and announces the dawn of
another beautiful morning here at the ocean...
where I have come once more to be refreshed
by the serenity of God's shore.

I stretch lazily in bed and smell the familiar
salt air that awakens my senses.
I push back the sun-drenched sheets
and look at the magnificent morning seascape
beyond the paint-chipped windowsill.

Puffs of brilliant white cotton dot the bluest of skies.
Seagulls dance in the morning air.
A distant ocean liner moves slowly on the horizon.

With all of this beauty surrounding me,

I want so much to feel joy and peace...

to appreciate this wondrous moment God has given me.

But my heart feels heavy today. Worries overwhelm me.

I feel sad...alone...troubled...and so tired that

it's even hard for me to pray.

And so I have come to the shore again...to take time out...

to listen to the soothing rhythm of the ocean...to seek

the presence of the Lord in the stillness and solitude here...

to try to regain peace and serenity in my soul.

I leave my bedroom, head downstairs, and push open

the rickety screen door. I pick up a faded beach towel

and an old sand pail and walk to the shore.

Lord, thank You for the gift of this brand new day

here at the ocean. I have many troubles and burdens

that are weighing me down. Help me give my cares

to You today, Lord, even for a moment,

so that I can be open to hear Your words...

so that I may be touched...refreshed...

strengthened...and renewed.

I put my towel and pail down on the glistening sand

and pass the remains of a sandcastle that probably stood tall

and proud only yesterday, before the tide rushed in.

I suddenly think of all the sandcastles my tiny hands

helped build when I was little. I remember

the countless buckets I would fill with wet sand

and then turn upside down to make a castle.

I remember shrieking with delight as I made

endless trips with my pail to the edge of the ocean,

trying to collect saltwater in my bucket

before the waves crashed in on me.

I remember sinking my eager fingers into the

wet sand to begin building my masterpiece.

I remember being totally preoccupied sculpting

my simple sand creations under brilliant

blue skies, focusing only on the immediate moment.

I remember feeling a sense of total, joy-filled

abandon. I had God's exquisite days to enjoy...

to live to the fullest. I remember feeling so

incredibly happy and free...down to the core of my soul.

I try hard to remember when I built my last sandcastle. Sadly enough, I can't remember. Was it when I was that little child? Perhaps. As the years have passed, why did I stop building sandcastles? In the stillness of this very moment, I think I know.

As the years have gone by, my joy in the moment

has been replaced with busyness...with worries

about tomorrow...and the next day...and the next.

I seem to race through my days, spending so much time

dwelling on yesterday and worrying about tomorrow

that I can't seem to see the sand in front of me.

I haven't stayed in the present long enough

to recognize all of the gifts around me.

No wonder I gave up building sandcastles so long ago.

I haven't allowed myself the gift of coming to the ocean

with an uncluttered mind...so that I could just play...

laugh...watch the seagulls...build sandcastles.

I have lost the joy of the moment that once was mine.

A tear falls from my eye as I sit down on the sand.

I push my toes into its comforting blanket of warmth.

I wrap my arms around my knees and put my head down.

19

Lord, my heart is so heavy today. You promise peace...

yet I am feeling stressed and anxious, even here at the ocean.

You promise to refresh me...yet I am exhausted

with the cares of life. I need Your help, Lord.

I want to believe that my life is in Your hands every moment.

Help me rest easy in that promise so that my spirit

can be refreshed...my heart renewed...

and my life can once again be filled with joy.

*Free my heart...if only for this moment...
from all that clutters it. Help still my mind...and body...
and heart...so that I may truly enjoy the gift
of this precious moment on Your shore.*

I hear a young child laughing, and I turn to see

a small boy running to the water's edge with his father.

The child is holding on to a multicolored kite...

the father has a ball of string in his hands.

I sit totally entranced in their joy

as the kite is lifted slowly from small hands

into the wind and carried on high.

*T*he father gradually lets the ball of string unwind.

I crane my neck and sit mesmerized as I watch the kite

soar, dip, and glide through the brilliant sky.

I am spellbound as I watch the kite's vivid colors

dance among the clouds.

And then suddenly I realize I am enjoying

a "sandcastle moment"...a rare instant in time

when I am totally lost in the joy of the present.

I am thinking of nothing but the beauty of this

young boy's kite as it soars above me.

For a brief time, I am feeling pure joy...

without a thought of yesterday...or tomorrow...

or the worries that fill my heart.

I am simply enjoying this moment to the fullest.

$\mathcal{I}$ suddenly realize that God places so many exquisite

"sandcastle moments" in my life every single day...

if I only take the time to recognize them...

to stay in the "now" and appreciate them...

to hold on to them...to cherish them.

Lord, help me not rush through each day

without taking the time to savor each precious moment

You give me...help me be refreshed by the everyday miracles...

the "sandcastle moments" all around me...

sharing time with a loved one

listening to the song of a bird

picking a handful of wild daisies

watching the dance of a butterfly

sitting in front of a crackling fire

watching the brilliance of a morning sunrise

enjoying the spectacle of an evening sunset

gazing up at a star-studded night sky

watching spring's first robins appear

watching the flight of a hummingbird at my feeder

holding the miracle of a newborn baby

watching the dance of a thousand fireflies as they light up the sky

listening to a gentle rain

swinging in a hammock under a giant oak tree

watching You paint the magic of a tree in autumn

smelling the fragrance of a rose

holding loved ones' hands around the table as we thank You for our many blessings

taking the time to say "I love you" to someone special

Lord, You give me so many opportunities for

"sandcastle moments" every single day.

Yet the busyness of my life finds me exhausted and spent

at the end of my days...oftentimes without having

taken the time to enjoy or appreciate even one

special moment from my day...

a day I will never be able to take back.

Lord, help slow me down...even for five minutes a day...

so that I might still my mind and calm my soul...

and appreciate the gifts and the magnificent beauty

around me before the tide comes in and washes them away.

*F*or life is so fleeting...so very fragile.

We never know whether this moment with a loved one

will be our last. May I always remember that this

is the only moment I have for sure. I can choose

to treasure it...and build a "sandcastle moment"...

or I can watch it disappear with the tides of time.

I look once again at the remains of yesterday's sandcastle

and I realize how very blessed sandcastle builders are.

They are the dream makers of the world,

for they take the time to create joy...

to make lasting magical memories out of simple

life experiences. When they build sandcastles,

they create joy-filled moments that often last for hours.

Sandcastle builders slow down when they see a rainbow.

They take the time to stop and appreciate its beauty.

They take time out from their day's hectic pace to lie

in summer's fresh green grass with their children.

They don't worry about when the tide will come and wash

a golden moment away. They are too busy happily

living that moment to the fullest and making

it worth remembering.

Sandcastle builders are young at heart
and leave behind to their loved ones
precious "sandcastle moments" as their legacy.

Life's little joy-filled moments are truly our greatest riches.

When my life is over, I hope I will be remembered

not for what I may have achieved, but for how many happy

"sandcastle moments" I may have helped create.

What good are all the riches the world can offer

if I haven't taken the time to have fun and build

a sandcastle along the way?

As I look at the remains of yesterday's sandcastle,

I know that some special people knelt by it...

their hearts youthful and free.

I can almost hear their joy and laughter...

I can almost feel their sense of fun...

adventure...creativity...and teamwork.

I know that the treasured moments

they shared on this shore

will last in their hearts forever.

*I*t doesn't matter who sandcastle builders are...

what they wear...or what they do.

All that matters is their ability

to get lost in a joy-filled moment.

It doesn't matter what the sandcastle looks like...

or how long it lasts. What matters is

the builder's desire to let the child come out

from his heart so that he may have fun

in the moment and make a lasting memory.

38

My heart is suddenly overflowing
with the love and magic and pure joy
of this very moment on God's shore.

Thank you, Lord, for the gift of today...

for helping me put down my troubles...

even for a moment...so that I could listen to You.

Thank You for reminding me of this precious moment...

of the sacredness of "now."

*T*hank You for showering me with beautiful

"sandcastle moments" every day.

Help me to live all of my days

with a bucketful of patience...playfulness...

and a childlike sense of adventure...

so that I may live each precious moment to the fullest.

Help me to dance and sing...laugh and play...

while this moment is still mine.

I stand up and go to the small remaining piece
of yesterday's sandcastle...and I am reminded again
of how very brief our blessings and
"sandcastle moments" really are.

Years have passed since my hands
have shaped a sandcastle.
Years have passed since I have
even wanted to build a sandcastle.
Somehow, this seems like
the very moment to begin again.

$\mathcal{I}$ sink to my knees next to the remains

of yesterday's sandcastle and, with the renewed spirit

of a young child...and with a heart filled with love...

and magic...and the pure joy of the moment...

I tip over a bucket of wet sand...

And begin to build.

One day at a time...this is enough.

Do not look back and grieve over yesterday,

for it is gone, and don't worry about tomorrow,

for it has not yet come. Just live in today

and make it so beautiful that it

will be worth remembering.

—Ida Scott Taylor